John Pendleton Kennedy

The Border States

Their Power and Duty in the Present Disordered Condition of the Country

John Pendleton Kennedy

The Border States
Their Power and Duty in the Present Disordered Condition of the Country

ISBN/EAN: 9783337041601

Printed in Europe, USA, Canada, Australia, Japan

Cover: Foto ©Suzi / pixelio.de

More available books at **www.hansebooks.com**

THE BORDER STATES,

THEIR POWER AND DUTY IN THE PRESENT DISOR-
DERED CONDITION OF THE COUNTRY.

THE BORDER STATES.

THE country is now, or, from all the tidings that reach us, must soon be compelled to accept the fact that South Carolina has seceded from the Union.

Whatever may be the right of secession, it is about to become a practical fact. South Carolina has announced her purpose, as far as it is in her power, to dissolve the Union. Other States belonging to that series which has lately assumed the designation of the Cotton States—as expressive of a peculiar affinity in interest and policy—are likely to follow her example. Alabama, which is, in some sense, the offspring of Carolina, her pupil and admiring disciple, has shown herself already too eager to precipitate herself into revolution to leave us any hope that she will hesitate to array herself on the side of her teacher. Perhaps we may still find some encouragement to a better augury, in the good sense and prudence of Georgia and the other States which have not been wholly possessed and fevered by that extraordinary contagion of frenzy which Carolina has spread through the lowlands of the South. But I confess my fears. The signs are against it. The chances are— for this event is not under the control of the sober judgment and wise estimate by which all matters of State should be directed—the chances are that passion will rule the hour, and that the revolution will move onward, swayed by the same rash impulses as those in which it originated.

We of the Border States, therefore, cannot too soon take counsel together, touching our own interest and duty in the new condition of affairs which is about to be forced upon us.

The question that now concerns us is—What position are we to assume in the beginning of the strife; where are we to place ourselves at the end of it?

Is it not very obvious that Virginia, Kentucky, Tennessee, Missouri, North Carolina and Maryland cannot, with any respect for their own dignity, with any regard for their own welfare, or with any security for their own peace, suffer themselves to be dragged into that track of revolution and civil war, of wild experiment and visionary project into which Carolina is endeavoring to force them?—These States are quite able to determine for themselves what griefs they suffer and what redress they require: they want no officious counsellor nor patronizing friend to tell them what it becomes them to do, either for the maintenance of their own honor or the promotion of their own advantage; they can hear with quiet scorn the taunt that they "have placed the Union above the rights and institutions of the South"—and hold at what it deserves the offensive rebuke "that no Southern State intent on vindicating her rights and preserving her institutions would go into conference with them."*

Every substantial hope of a successful issue out of the afflictions of the country, produced equally by the wickedness of Northern fanaticism, and the intemperate zeal of secession, depends upon the calm and earnest wisdom of the Border States. That they will be true to the duties of the crisis, no one who has studied their character can for a moment doubt.

However the lowland States may now slight their counsels and disparage their patriotism, it is a most weighty and significant truth, for the consideration of the leaders of the projected revolution, that the Border States are at this time the most authentic representatives of the conservative power of the Union. Their various and equal relations to the North, the South and the West, their social organization

---

* See the Charleston Mercury of November 19, where this language is held to Virginia and the other Border States, in the editorial headed "Southern Conference—too late."

for the support of every interest connected with good government and permanent peace, their internal strength, and above all, their healthful tone of opinion towards the preservation of constitutional right and resistance against wrong, point them out as the safest and best arbiters in the present difficulties of the country. Whatever there is of real vigor in the slaveholding communities, exists in *them* and is derived in greatest degree, by others, from *their* sympathy and alliance. Without them, we may affirm, that no confederacy of Slave States, at all worthy of respect and consideration as an independent power, can possibly be formed.

The attempt, whenever made, will speedily prove itself to be a most unhappy failure.

The Border States have a better right to claim a hearing, just now, than any other member of the Union. Indeed, until *they* have spoken, it would almost seem to savor of an unbecoming officiousness on the part of any other State to put itself in the van to raise an outcry of wrong or to dictate the measure of remedy.

Whilst these States have always manifested a just and becoming sensibility to their rights, connected with the employment of slave labor, and have shared in the common indignation of the South against the malignant hostility of certain sections of the Northern people; whilst they have been the chief and almost only sufferers from the inroads of organized abolitionists who have stealthily abstracted their slaves in numbers, whose value may be reckoned at little less than a million of dollars a year, whilst, indeed, it may be said, that these States are the only portions of the slaveholding region which have any direct, immediate or definite interest, worthy of special consideration, in the vexed questions touching the present or the future of slavery in the United States—that is to say, in the question of emigration to the territories, the rendition of fugitives, and the organization of new States—they have, nevertheless, shown themselves, in all contingencies, the confident and considerate assertors of their rights in the mode ordained by the Constitution, and at all times the determined friends of the

Union. They have never yet felt an aggression which they did not believe more effectively to be repelled by the due exercise of the power of the government, than by retreat before the aggressor and resort to a covert revolution that seeks to legalize its action by taking the name of secession.

They certainly cannot be expected now, with the painful conviction which passing events are creating in their minds—that the Union itself is the chief grievance which stirs the hostility of those who are most active in raising a banner of revolt, and that the assaults upon the property of slave-holders, of which they, the Border States, have so much cause to complain, are but the pretext to cover a concealed design of portentous mischief—they cannot be expected now, with such a conviction, to renounce the wisdom of their accustomed trust in the law, and allow themselves to be persuaded or beguiled into a desertion at once of the Constitution which they have always respected, or of the Union which they have always revered. Their course is too plainly marked out to them by the incidents of the day to admit of any such fatal aberration as that. They are not blind to the fact that the present crisis has been forced upon the country with a haste that allowed no halt, chiefly because its contrivers feared the sound of that voice from the Border States, which they knew would speak peace to the troubled waves of strife, and would reach the heart of hosts of loyal citizens in the very bosom of the commotion,—citizens, alas, now bereft of their loyalty by the force of the tempest of revolution that has swept over them.

If thus Carolina and her comrades are lost—all is not lost. There is space for arbitrament still left which may, at least, secure an opportunity for mediation, and I would hope an eventual settlement, that may, perhaps, include even those who are at present the most resolute in their recusancy. Carolina now repeats defiantly that all chance of her return is gone forever. I would fain believe that affairs may be conducted into such a channel, as to awaken in her a better view of her own future.

It is very important that the country should consider the true character of the danger that threatens it. The public mind is sadly at fault upon this point. There has been a singular concurrence of accident and design to lead even sensible and observant men off from the perception of the real causes of this disturbance; and a not less singular exhibition of practised skill in the address with which the popular masses, in the region of the commotion, have been enlisted in an enterprise, of the scope and consequences of which they had neither the leisure to examine nor the temper to comprehend.

The public for the most part believe that the impending revolution grows out of the organization of the Republican party, and that the recent election presented the culminating point at which that organization could no longer be endured with safety to the Southern States.

Unfortunate as that election is, not only in its result, but in all the stages of its progress from the day of the Chicago Convention, down to that of its consummation—unfortunate for the tranquility of the country, and for the predominance it has given to certain men and certain political sects—it is not less unfortunate for the opportunity it has afforded to the accomplishment of designs long nourished, which have been held in suspense only to await a juncture favorable to their success.

The graver and more thoughtful portions of the community have recognized with no little pain, the steady growth in some sections of the South, for many years past, of a disposition, in the leaders of Southern opinion, to undervalue both the strength and the beneficence of the Union. It belongs to the school of doctrine of which South Carolina is the head, to imbue the people with the idea that the State Sovereignty has the first claim to the allegiance of the citizen, and that no more is due to the National Sovereignty than may be found not incompatible with this superior duty; that to support the State, right or wrong, in whatever demand it may make in conflict with the Federal authority, is the natural and most proper exhibition of a becoming State pride.

This school has also been the source of certain theories touching the structure and aims of our government, which, although founded, as we conceive, on mistaken views, both of the facts of its history and of the necessary conditions upon which alone any government of a population so extensive as ours is practicable, could not but lead in time to angry dissension and inveterate sectional prejudice.

Conspicuous amongst these theories are two which have taken a deep hold upon the Southern mind. To their influence we may trace no small amount of the discontent which has weakened the attachment of some of the Southern States to the Union ; and which has also led to the large acceptance they have given to the efficacy and lawfulness of that extreme measure which Carolina now proposes as the proper remedy for the evils which threaten her in common with all other slaveholding States.

The first of these theories asserts that the Federal Government was constructed on the basis of an equilibrium of power between the Free and Slave States, which equilibrium was designed to be forever preserved in all the vicissitudes of the future. The failure to preserve it is consequently regarded as a violation of a fundamental compromise.

The second is that which affirms all import duties to be an exclusive tax upon the Planting States, by virtue of which they are burdened with the charge of the entire support of Government.

I might add to these, that other theory from the same school, and equally questionable, which conceives the ever present and effective remedy for all real or fancied griefs, to exist in the doctrine of a lawful right of secession.

Without stopping to debate the soundness of these several tenets, I refer to them as presenting the real germs of the discontent which has been smouldering at the heart of Carolina for years, and as suggesting the true explanation of that phenomenon which puzzles the whole nation at this day, the activity, namely, and apparent supererogatory zeal with which Carolina has first, and before all her sister States of the South, flung herself into the arena to vindicate them by revolution and destruction of the Union.

These teachings have been long silently undermining her attachment to the Federal Government, and have at last wholly obliterated in her that sentiment of reverence for the Union which our forefathers inculcated, with a religious earnestness, as the foundation of American Nationality.

It is a fact of common observation that the present generation of public men in Carolina have been educated in ominous familiarity with the thought of disunion. It has been the toy of their childhood, the weapon of their age of active life. It has gathered edge and strength in a long and petulant quarrel with the National Government. It has, at last, taken visible shape in the instant, defiant act of secession.

Carolina frankly avows the Union to be an obstruction to her prosperity. That is not the sentiment alone of to-day. It has, for years past, been her earnest conviction that the Federal Government, administered on the principles most accordant with the wishes of a large number of the States, is not compatible with her welfare. She, therefore, thinks she has a right to retire from the compact and assume the position of an independent nation.

She, moreover, thinks that it is altogether consistent with her duty to her sister States with whom she has had no ground of quarrel, to propagate her own discontent amongst such of them as she may deem useful to her project and by persuasion, solicitation and convention to lure them out of the Union into alliance with herself.

The short compend of these claims, is expressed in the postulate—a right, at her pleasure, to dissolve the Union.

Every one has heard and read how pertinaciously she has argued this right in every forum open to her service.

Persuading herself that she has this right, to be used whenever she thinks proper, she deduces from it, quite logically, the right to meditate over every problem of possible contingencies which might, in the evolution of events, be turned to her advantage. As for instance, whether she

2

would not thrive better if certain prohibitions of the Constitution were removed? Would it be to her benefit to make Charleston a free port?—to negotiate a commercial treaty with England?—with France?—to make a new Confederacy within the territory of the Union?—to open and re-establish the African slave trade?—a hundred such questions which she may deem fit to consider and determine whilst she remains a member of the Confederacy—and the objects of which, if she cannot accomplish them in the* Union, she thinks it unreasonable to be denied the privilege of accomplishing by secession from the Union.

I would not willingly misrepresent Carolina—much less, speak in derogation of her really high and admirable qualities of character. There is no community of the same size, I believe, in the world that has produced a larger share of distinguished men. There is no society in the United States more worthy of esteem for its refinement, its just and honorable sentiment, and its genial virtues.

The men of Carolina are distinguished by the best qualities of attractive manhood. They are brave, intelligent and frank. They speak what they think, and they mean what they say. They are the last people in this Union we should desire to part with—notwithstanding their strange insulation of opinion, their exclusive philosophies, and, what they must pardon us for thinking, their political sophisms !

In these sundry meditations of theirs, they have long since struck upon one or more of the conclusions which I have hinted above—the opinion, namely, that they would do better in a Southern Confederacy than in the Union made by their forefathers. And having come to that conclusion, they have wrought themselves to the sober—or rather let me say, the vehement conclusion that they are the most oppressed people of Christendom.

In 1832, their oppression existed in the unhappy fact that the Government persisted in continuing a policy originally supported, if not demanded, by Carolina herself, which was founded upon the most approved economical science of that day, and the practice of all enlightened nations,—the encouragement of the domestic industry of the country. As a remedy for this grief, they proposed secession and dissolution of the Union—but not being unanimous in that conclusion, they resorted to the milder process of nullification.

How many times since that, they have determined to dissolve the Union, it would be tedious to enumerate. But, in 1851, their grievances grew so intolerable, through the admission of California into the Union, with a constitution made according to its own view of what was best for it, that all the altars were lighted up once more with an unusual conflagration of the never dying flames of liberty and independence.

What was the extent of suffering then, and what the peculiar *gravamen* of that day, we may learn from their own oracles.

In order that I may speak from the book, I will quote some passages—almost too long, but still so full of matter, that I am unwilling to shorten them, from the chosen and authentic expounder of Southern opinion,—The Southern Quarterly Review.

In an article of the October number of 1851, entitled, "South Carolina, her present attitude and future action,"— from the sum of much grave advice touching revolution, and hinting, amongst other things, at the passage of bills of attainder and the use of the axe, I extract the following exposition of wrongs and suggestions of remedy.

"But the people of South Carolina"—says the Reviewer— "have not yet entirely forgotten the angry feelings growing out of the war of the Revolution. Well, then, let them read over the Declaration of Independence, and compare the wrongs recited there, with those we now endure. What was the *actual* grievance then? What is it now? Then they 'augured misgovernment at a distance.' Now, the evil is upon them, *and ten fold greater evil than the most far-seeing politician of that day anticipated from British tyranny.* One, and but one of the luxuries of the rich was taxed not more than five per cent. Now, every necessary of life which she does not produce at home, *is taxed at an average rate of not less than thirty per cent.* Then *Old* England claimed the right to exact from her a portion of the revenue necessary for the support of the British Empire, while the amount expended for the benefit of South Carolina very far exceeded all that she was called on to contribute. Now, *New* England requires her together with a few of her uncomplaining and acquiescent sisters *to furnish the whole revenue of the Union,* no part of which comes back to them, except in the shape of bribes to such as are willing to sell themselves into the service of their enemies, for Texas scrip and the emoluments of office."

*   *   *   *   *   *   *

——"She (Massachusetts) was wronged. She was outlawed and her port of Boston was shut. *We* took up arms in *her* quarrel. It was hardly our own. But we made it our own. It was for her that our Moultrie, Marion, Pickens and Sumpter fought in defence of our firesides, against an enemy whom our zeal in her behalf brought upon us. From Ninety-Six to Charleston our country is full of monuments of our efforts in her cause. It was for her the gallant Hayne died a felon's death ; and the requital of that sacrifice is, to threaten the like doom to his descendants should they be as bold in defence of our own rights as he was then in defence of hers. We separated ourselves from *Old* England because the port of Boston was shut up. Should we now separate ourselves from *New* England, we hear from Boston itself that the port of Charleston is to be shut up." *   *   *

After this, we have a glimpse of the remedy proposed for these oppressions.

"What is there at this day antagonistic between the interests of Great Britain and those of South Carolina? Is not each the consumer of all the other's productions, reciprocally? Is not their relation like that of the sexes, each necessary to the other. And shall South Carolina, like the Circassian slave, continue shut up in the harem of a brutal and sordid tyrant, when a generous lover is waiting to make her his honored wife, and to establish her in wealth and comfort and freedom and all the dignity of a Christian matron?''

* * * * * * *

——''With all her professions of friendship Massachusetts hates England with an inextinguishable, because an *interested* hatred. They are rivals in commerce. They are rivals in manufactures. An especial object of rivalry is the commerce of the Southern States, and hence Massachusetts does all she can to keep alive their old animosities and to prevent the growth of any sympathy between us and England. Hence she excites the impertinent clamors of English abolitionists. What for? *Can they interfere with our institutions? No. They can but make us angry.*'' * * *

It is a mistake, as we may gather from what follows, to suppose that England is really opposed to slavery. Her professed aversion to it is a mere stratagem to allay her own discontents. Her object is to keep her own work people quiet, by inducing them to believe that the world contains more wretched beings than themselves.

——''They (her West India possessions) have become a burthen to her. They continually harass her with well-founded complaints and demand some indemnity in the way of protection to their sugar in the English market. But this is oppressive to her people at home, and especially to the manufacturing operative, to whom coarse sugars are a necessary of life. *To reconcile him to this, nothing so ready as an appeal to his sympathies with his brother slave on this side of the Atlantic; and he, poor wretch, shut up in the work-house, the factory or the mine, readily believes that the condition of the negro slave must be 'a lower depth in that lowest deep' with the horrors of which he is so familiar.*''

* * * * * * *

—— ''Let but South Carolina, *even alone,* set up for herself, and establish such commercial relations with Great Britain as would be best for both parties, how long would it be before Great Britain would see her interest *in permitting and encouraging and aiding Jamaica and her other West India*

Islands, to form one State, and Demerara another, and to enter into confederacy with South Carolina?"

And as a matter of course, a new slave trade from America would be established by the aid of England in this hopeful project.

"Getting slaves from the continent, they would need no more protection, and all clamor about 'slave-grown sugar' would cease forever. Entering the ports of England under a moderate revenue tariff, the sugar would find its way to the operative at half its present price, and the poor woman wasted and worn by her twelve hours of unceasing toil, would not be obliged to deny herself the cheering influence of her indispensable cup of tea—her only luxury and not her least necessary."

It is with such food as this that the mind of warm-hearted, impulsive, credulous Carolina is fed to nurture this project of disunion!

Extravagant as this declamation may appear to a calm reader, capable of estimating, at their true value, the happy certainties that belong to the present and the future of a State in the American Union, and the dreadful uncertainties that impend over separation, even in its most hopeful reckoning, it nevertheless expresses the views and expectations of that portion, at least, of the community in which it is uttered, who have been allowed "to instruct the Southern mind and fire the Southern heart" for the momentous struggle which is now inaugurated in South Carolina. In that aspect it is worthy of special notice at this time.

It demonstrates what I have already intimated, that the secession movement is not the suddenly inspired project of the present day; that it does not grow out of the events of the recent canvass and election, nor even primarily out of that agitation of slavery, which constitutes the flagrant cause of disturbance in the Border States.

If we analyse this paper we shall see that the aggressions of the Northern States upon the peaceful employment of Southern labor, is scarcely referred to at all: that the real and predominant grievance complained of is found in the old question of taxation. The support of the government by imports, regulated to the revenue standard, is presented as an abuse tenfold more oppressive than all the tyranny that led to the revolution of seventy-six. The State of South Carolina and her few uncomplaining sisters are represented as groaning under the intolerable burthen of paying the *whole revenue* of the Federal Government and getting nothing in return. This is a repetition of the grief of 1832, when the country was mystified with that most inscrutable of all revelations, "the forty bale theory,"—and which so far prevailed in the philosophy of the National Councils, as finally to secure the triumph of what is claimed to be the free trade adjustment of 1846,—which adjustment, it seems now, is no more satisfactory than the protective system it displaced.

It is, also, worthy of note, that the rabid abolitionism of England, of which so much has been said of late in the way of denunciation, and which, in fact, is quite as mischievous to Southern peace as the fanaticism it encourages in New England, is regarded not only as harmless, but even' as not standing in the way of a most cordial alliance with Great Britain. The reviewer actually apologises for this little indiscretion in the expected ally, and treats it with a temper of good sense which might be commendably adopted in regard to the same transgression at home—"can they interfere with our institutions? No. They can but make us angry."

We have a further exposition of the policy of disunion, in the imagination of a Southern Confederacy composed of Jamaica, and other British West India Islands and Demerara,—or, I suppose, the reviewer meant British Guyana on the South American continent—to which may now be added, as a more recent development of the grandeur of the contemplated republic, the conception of similar accretions embracing Cuba, San Domingo, Mexico and perhaps Central America. This Confederacy, if we mistake not the significance of many ill-suppressed hints from indiscreet friends, is to be rendered still more magnificent and bountiful of blessings, still more attractive to the contemplation of man-kind by the aid of a productive commerce in African slaves, which seems to be not the least winning feature in the project.

These are the fervid dreams of the contrivers of disunion. For such fantasies as these, our great Republic, the matured product of so much thought and suffering is to be rent asunder, just at the era when we fondly imagined it to have risen to that height in the estimation of mankind which gave it an assured position amongst the proudest empires of history. For such impracticable conceits as these, it is to be resolved into discordant fragments whose perpetual jars may illustrate the saddest moral of blighted hopes the world has ever known!

We might bear this melancholy lot with submissive patience, as the chastisement of offended heaven if we could believe there was any cause to give it the semblance of an unavoidable affliction : if, indeed, it did not spring from the merest wantonness of a temper engendered by too much pros-perity—or ingratitude to God for blessings too profusely be-stowed to be valued.

There is something in the time and in the pretext chosen for this great work of mischief that peculiarly provokes remark. The pretext is the general agitation of the South-ern mind by the Northern triumph over slavery. What quarrel there is that grows out of this, is, as we have affirmed, the just and proper quarrel of the Border States. That quarrel does not necessarily, and most probably would not, lead to a breach of the Union. Firm remonstrance and wise counsel, aided by that strong attachment to the govern-ment, which, both North and South, lives in the heart of millions of conservative men may bring a truce,—which indeed is already begun,—auspicious to reflection and the settlement of all these differences. It is no difficult matter in this breathing space, when considerate citizens are brought face to face with honest purpose of peace, to frame an ad-justment in which future repose and sufficient pledge against the renewal of strife may be obtained.

It is just at such a time as this, in the interval when reason, judgment and fraternal affection are beginning to infuse a benignant influence over the disturbed mind of the country,—that the master spirits of the new Confederacy rush to the verge of the gulf and drive their maddened partizans to the dreadful leap that makes recall impossible. They pursue their desperate course without a moment's pause, neither looking back, nor taking breath; deaf to all entreaty of friends, and blind to all sights but the visions that rise in the distant prospect. There they behold their Arcadia, with its phantoms of untold wealth, its free ports, its untaxed commerce, its illimitable cotton fields, its flattering alliances, its swarms of reinforcement from the shores of Africa. To reach this promised land, the only condition of the enterprise is to press forward with fiery haste and outrun the speed of the peace-makers.

In 1851, Carolina pursued her scheme of secession as resolutely as she does at this day, and only failed through the prudence of those who refused to accompany her. Her purpose was as ripe then, her hopes as high, as now. Yet, at that epoch there was no fear of a Republican President. There was then no question of intervention or non-intervention, no debate of equal rights in the territories, no Kansas, no John Brown. In the absence of all these, she had nothing but California and the Compromise to disturb her repose. Yet her sufferings, as she declared, were too intolerable to be borne. Let her speak for herself. It was the Union she could not endure. "Welcome as summer showers to the sun parched earth"—was the wail of her Quarterly of that time. "Welcome as Heaven's free air to the heart-sick tenant of a dungeon, would come to us the voice of freedom, the word, the deed which would tend to burst our bonds, and in earnest faith contribute to the disruption of this proud fabric (once beautiful, but now rotten to the core) which, under the name of Union, threatens to crush us beneath its unholy power."

We cannot believe that this complicated tissue of extravagant projects, of fancied ills, of illusory imaginations, has

3

taken any absolute hold upon the judgment of the really sound intellect of Carolina. The many wise and patriotic men, who have adorned the councils of the nation as well as of the State; the many whom we know in private life, distinguished for good sense, clear perception of duty and the highest order of ability, forbid the belief that, when this extraordinary tempest of passion shall subside, they will not be at hand to lead back the State to the path into which her true renown and her best interests invite her. We are aware of the bewildering force of popular excitement lashed into fury by the eloquence and the arts of ambitious leaders; how irresistibly it seizes upon impressible and ardent natures, how strangely it, some times, overmasters the discretion of the wise. But we also know that, in the very highest rage of its sweep it is never without an earnest and silent dissent in the bosoms of grave and interested spectators who dare not, or, in the hopelessness of a hearing, will not even whisper a remonstrance against the heady current of the multitude. They abide their time. We believe that at this moment, there is in Carolina many a sad and watchful citizen anxiously awaiting the day when the collapse of this overstrained ardor shall present an occasion to speak a word for the Union and for the stricken fortunes of the State, without fear of that stern and angry derision which now compels him to hold his peace.

But I leave this topic to recur to the question,—What is the proper duty of the Border States, looking to the contingencies of this unhappy strife?

Obviously they cannot, in the present circumstances, cast their lot with Carolina. They cannot adopt either her passion or her policy. They can go into no confederation of the lowland States, organized on the principles and motives which they have so much reason to fear now direct and stimulate the ambition of Carolina. Then let them say so at once.

Let them say to her and to those who may unite their fortunes with hers, that, deeply deploring a separation which they would make every just or generous sacrifice to avert,—a separation that is forced upon them by a profound conviction that it is the only expedient left open to them to guard against still greater evils—they must submit to it as the inevitable destiny of their position.

The Border States have their own welfare to protect, their own injuries to redress. They believe that both of these may be accomplished within the Union. They have no issue with any section of the Union, but that which springs from the hostility engendered in the minds, and manifested in the public action, of certain portions of the Free States. They have no hopes or fears which may not be encouraged or quieted by the lawful and orderly administration of the constitutional powers of the Federal Government. They regard that government as the wisest scheme that can be devised for the rule of this nation. They can never abandon it until experience shall convince them that it is no longer capable to resist its perversion by faction, or to protect the rights of every State and citizen.

That experience they have not yet had.

They acknowledge that in the resolution of the Union into fragments, which may be the possible result of the present disturbances, a contingency may be presented to them in which they will be compelled to choose their own lot.

Their first and greatest desire is to avert that contingency and to restore peace and universal concord amongst the whole sisterhood of States.

Supposing these to be the sentiments of the Border States, which, from every authentic indication, I cannot doubt, I venture to suggest for their consideration,—

The expediency, as a preliminary measure, of holding, at an early day, an informal Conference to be conducted by one or more distinguished citizens from each of the Border States, and from such of the other Southern States as may be opposed to secession in the present state of affairs—these to be selected by the Executive of each State—for the purpose of determining on a course of joint action to be recommended to the adoption of the whole number.

To such a conference I would submit the following propositions:

1. The propriety of making an earnest appeal to the seceding States to retrace their steps and await the result of the measures proposed for the establishment of general harmony: with a declaration that if this appeal be unsuccessful, they, the Border States, will be compelled to decline entering into a Southern Confederacy as now proposed by South Carolina and her allies in secession.

2. That if the secession of South Carolina be followed by that of Alabama or any other State, and a serious breach of the Union be thus established, it will then be incumbent on the Border States and the other Southern States concurring with them, to take measures for their own security, by demanding from the Free States a revisal of all topics of complaint between them and the Slave States, and the adoption of such stipulations on both sides as shall be satisfactory to each for the determination and protection of Southern rights, and for the restoration of harmony.

These stipulations would, of course, become the subject of a negotiation with the Free States: a negotiation which should be conducted in a frank and conciliatory spirit, through such agencies as the parties may arrange.

I think it would be just to both parties, and would be likely to meet the general approval of the country, to direct these stipulations to the following points:

The re-establishment of the Missouri line and its extension to the Pacific, as an easy, practicable mode of settling the territorial question on a basis with which the people are familiar.

The adjustment of the question of the rendition of fugitive slaves:

By such modifications of the provisions of the act of Congress on that subject, as shall remove every reasonable objection to it, compatible with its efficient adaptation to its purpose: and by an agreement on the part of the Free States, to execute it in good faith, and to repeal all laws heretofore passed with a view to its obstruction:

This, coupled with an engagement, in case any State should find itself unable, by reason of the repugnance of the people to the execution of the law, to deliver up the fugitive—then, to be allowed and required, by way of alternative, to make a just indemnity to the owner, under such regulations as may be devised.

The settlement of the question in regard to the admission of New States on the foundation at present adopted, of leaving each territory to form a State Constitution in accordance with its own wishes.

Finally, a pledge to be given by the Free States to exert their influence, as far as possible, to discourage discussions of slavery in a tone offensive to the interests of the slaveholding States; and to endeavor to procure legislative enactments against preparations for assault on the peace of these States, either by individuals or organized bodies.

If there be any of the provisions proposed in these stipulations which may require an amendment of the Constitution—an agreement should be made to propose and support it.

3. If these stipulations can be obtained—Then the Border States and concurring States of the South, which have not seceded, shall retain their present position in the Union.

But in the adverse event of these stipulations, or satisfactory equivalents for them, being refused, the Border States and their allies of the South who may be disposed to act with them, will be forced to consider the Union impracticable, and to organize a separate Confederacy of the Border States, with the association of such of the Southern and Free States as may be willing to accede to the proposed conditions.

4. When this programme of action, or such substitute for it as the Conference may devise, shall be adopted, it should be submitted, through the respective Executives of the States represented in the Conference, to the people of each, to be acted upon in a General Convention of those States, called by the direction and appointment of their several Legislatures.

5. That pending the whole course of this proceeding, the Border States and those concurring with them, shall engage to prevent, by all the means in their power, any attempt on the part of the Federal Government or of any State or States to coerce the seceding States by armed force into submission.

It may be a proper subject for such a Conference, as I have proposed, to consider whether it would not be useful, in any event—even in that of the single secession of South Carolina, before any other State shall have followed her,—to offer the Border States as mediators in the present unhappy differences, and to endeavor to procure, for the benefit of all, the stipulations I have described above, or some other pacific arrangement of the same character and object.

If the Border States can be brought into combination in the manner pointed out by those propositions, it is easy to perceive that they must immediately become the masters of the position from which the whole national controversy is most likely to be controlled. They will not only hold the general peace in their hands, by their authority to persuade an abstinence from all attempts at coercion; but they will also be regarded and respected on all sides, as the natural and appropriate medium through which the settlement of all differences is eventually to be obtained.

By taking the ground, at the earliest moment, that they cannot unite in the scheme of the Southern Confederacy, and that, if separation should, at last, after all efforts to avert it, be imposed upon them by an inexorable necessity from which there is no escape, they will be compelled to construct a Confederacy of their own, in which they may be able to associate with themselves, perhaps the whole body of the Middle and Western States—if they, the Border States, shall firmly and dispassionately take this ground, such a deter- · mination cannot but suggest to the seceding States the gravest motive to pause in their meditated career, and to await an opportunity for further conference and debate. It will then be for these States to inquire with more deliberation than they have yet given to the subject, what will be the strength and capacity for self-support of a Confederacy unsustained by the power and resource of such communities as those which decline the alliance. When that question comes to be seriously discussed by them it will present many new and momentous considerations which have not yet been canvassed.

The popular notion of a united South is but an impracticable fancy. A united South is a more uncertain problem than even the support of the present Union under the difficulties that now surround it.

I think it will appear to any careful explorer of the subject, that if the fifteen States South of Mason and Dixon's line, were to enter into a Confederacy amongst themselves, such an organization would speedily prove itself to be more productive of dissension than the present Union has been during the last twenty years.

The policy prefigured by the seceding States is in many points, wholly repugnant to the views and interests of the Border States.

These latter could never be reconciled to be made accomplices in the disgrace and guilt of a restoration of the slave trade, they would never undertake to face the indignation of Christendom which would arise upon its revival—much less would they agree to involve themselves in the expense and burthen of the wars that it would inevitably provoke.

The Border States would scarcely less endure the commercial system, so often and conspicuously insisted on by Carolina and her comrades in secession, by which free ports are demanded and the consequent necessity of a public revenue resting upon direct taxation.

They could not be persuaded into that expansive policy of annexation and conquest which has dazzled the imagination of the South and tormented the ambition of its people, in persistent forays upon neighboring States and perpetual schemes of acquisition.

The Border States exhibit within their area a representation of almost every interest and pursuit in the Union. They are thriving and vigorous communities, with most prolific resources for every species of industry. Their agriculture furnishes an abundant supply of the sustenance of life, with a large surplus for external commerce. The region occupied by these States embraces also a wide area adapted to the culture of hemp and flax, tobacco and cotton. It abounds in mineral wealth, in water power, in pasturage, in cattle, sheep, horses—in all the elements of the most diversified manufacturing industry. Its healthful climate, its robust population and its cheap means of livelihood are singularly favorable to the growth and prosperity of the mechanic arts, the multiplication of villages and the gradual increase of thrifty and industrious workmen in every department of handicraft—invariably the best indications of the progress of a State to wealth and power.

Beginning at the Cities of Baltimore, Richmond and Norfolk on the Atlantic, and extending over a broad domain studded with flourishing inland towns, it ends at the City of St. Louis on the Missouri, presenting throughout the series, every facility for a wide and profitable commerce, already furnished with rail roads, canals and navigable rivers.

Here are all the elements necessary to the organization of the polity of a first class power. In extent of territory, in resource, in population, it may take rank amongst the master States which, in any new combinations of the fragments of our once happy Union, broken by the madness of faction, may hereafter be gathered from the wreck.

In the worst event that may happen, therefore, greatly as every old-fashioned lover of the Union may deplore the necessity for such a work, here are the ready materials for the construction of a new nation able to protect the welfare of its people, secure their peaceful pursuit of happiness, and furnish a safe refuge to all who may flee to it to escape the disorders and distractions of the time.

It is a sad speculation which forces us to the computation of the resources of any section of our present Union, with a view to the exhibition of its capacity for independent existence; but when the vision of a united South is conjured up to our contemplation, as a possible or impending reality, we are compelled to face and question it.

I have therefore looked at the character of the Border States, to shew how incompatible their interests are likely to prove with the policy which is deemed essential to other sections of the South. It must be apparent from even this brief examination, that communities of such different pursuits, and marked by such variant conditions, would scarcely find, in political alliance with the projected Southern Confederacy, that harmony of interests which is essential to the prosperity of both.

The four or five States now reputed to be most likely to enter into compact with Carolina, may be described as chiefly representing one vast cotton field. The whole region embraced by them is, in all physical quality, if we except Georgia, thoroughly homogeneous. Its business is planting: It has no mechanic art and but few manufactures. Its rural inhabitants are divided between numerous proprietors of the soil and their slaves—the proprietors, in great degree, migratory, the slaves stationary—thus necessarily creating, in many locations, a great preponderance of slave population. Its productions are singularly valuable as one of the most indispensable wants of mankind, and readily exchangeable into money. This exchange is made through an active factorage that has built up prosperous cities and created a large commerce. So far as this commerce is concerned with the planting region, it is reduced into a simple system of transactions in the great staple of the country—a commerce without variety of resource, and too dependent upon the accidents of a single product and the vicissitudes of season, to support a costly mercantile marine, and which is therefore compelled to seek its transportation from foreign and friendly sources. Such a commerce, we must perceive, is peculiarly exposed, not only to damage, but utter overthrow by the occurrence of war. In its overthrow, the whole resource of the country is destroyed. This is the common and inevitable weakness of all merely agricultural countries.

If Louisiana, shaken from her balance by the fervor of the moment, could be persuaded to join this Confederacy, she would contribute, it is true, not only another resource in her product of sugar, but a great commercial mart of commanding importance in the trade of the world. It might nevertheless be questioned whether even so valuable an acquisition as this, would, in the end, turn out to be a permanent accession of strength. The prosperity of the City of New Orleans is so essentially united with the fortunes of the West—in fact, so entirely dependent upon them, as to suggest many possibilities of collision, both on the part of the City and State, with the policy of the Government to whose control they would have surrendered themselves. Indeed, with the obvious motives for hesitation, which must occur to the intelligent judgment of Lousiana, against the wisdom of entering into the proposed Confederacy, it is scarcely to be presumed that she may be seduced, even by the passionate solicitations of her present anger against Northern aggression, into a measure, in its best aspect, so doubtful ; in its apparent probabilities, so rash.

She cannot slight the consideration that the adverse possession of a great seat of trade at the mouth of the Mississippi, may furnish in the future, as it has done in the past, a fruitful source of quarrel between the power that holds it, and the numerous commonwealths upon the banks of the river and its tributaries, which now claim its free and uninterrupted use, together with its depots, at all times and in all contingencies: that there is no form of agreement or treaty which can afford complete and invariable protection to this enjoyment: none that would probably be regarded as an adequate equivalent for the surrender of the right which has been acquired by purchase out of the common treasure, for the benefit of these claimants.

Will not these reflections suggest a pregnant inquiry whether the defence of this mart by a confederacy foreign to the claimants, may not prove a charge too costly to be compensated even by the unquestionably great advantages of such a possession? Does it presignify no danger that, in the vexatious emergencies of future years, there may be provoked a new motive in Louisiana, for *secession* from a confederacy that is to be built upon a full recognition of that doctrine? In view of these possibilities and many others that experience may bring to light, may we not assume that Louisiana will prudently weigh the question of her own permanent peace and prosperity, before she takes the step to which she is now invited? Will it not be equally well for the new Confederacy to deliberate upon the point whether such a possession may not be as much a source of weakness as of strength?

Looking back to the elements,—with that notable exception, to which I have already adverted,—which are expected to compose this Confederacy; to its people and pursuits, and the peculiar character of a large portion of its population; to its deficiency in mechanic art, its defective supply of the staff of life; to the influence of its climate ; to its entire destitution of the means to build and man ships, and to many other disabilities which will occur in any review of its resources, we cannot but think that this fancied New Atlantis, which has so possessed the imagination of its votaries, will, upon trial, prove itself to be the most defenceless, and in a significant sense, the weakest of independent nations.

It may have some hope of rising above this condition by the accession of the State of Georgia. If that vigorous commonwealth, in an hour of blindness to its own happy destiny in this Union, should fall into the fatal error of joining in this alliance, it will be, as every one must admit, a constituent of real strength in the Confederacy. Georgia would then arise to the unenviable supremacy of being the only solid and trusty support of the whole fabric. She has already, under the auspices of a Union which has conferred nothing but blessings upon her, advanced beyond all her compeers of the South, to the position of a truly powerful and commanding commonwealth. Surely, before she takes this fatal step, she will meditate over the prosperity of her admirable effort in the establishment of manufactures, her multiplying towns and villages, her fertile and healthy uplands, her rapid growth in peaceful arts, and her thousand capabilities of ever-varied industry, and anxiously and coolly weigh the question, whether she should put all these in jeopardy by submitting them to the domination of such a policy as the new Confederacy will offer her. But if, in full view of these admonitions, she chooses to be led into the first movement towards this combination, may we not hope that in a calmer moment than the present, she will retrace her steps and once more place her better destiny under the guardianship of the Stars and Stripes— the only symbol worthy of her fortunes and her hopes?

Georgia has not yet left us. Let us trust to the clear judgment and earnest patriotism of her hosts of friends to the Union, and to the eloquent and manly counsel of her sons, that she will move with more deliberate pace, and in company with more temperate comrades, along the path of conciliation and trial, before she ventures to lend a hand to the demolition of the government under which she has grown to her present stature. And if that day of destruction must ever come, let her be found among the ruins, with kindred congenial to her own nature, employed in the task of gathering the fragments of our broken Union together for reconstruction and renewal of its ancient harmony.

Texas is looked to as a component of the New Confederacy. Her lot, if dissolution be a settled fact, and a general *sauve qui peut* should compel her to decide upon her whereabout, I presume, would be, once more, to raise her banner of the Lone Star. She is a young nation, quite able to take care of herself. She exists as a portion of the American Union by a simple resolution of Congress. A dissolution repeals that act and remits her to her original position. She becomes again a detached and independent power; and, in that event, may wisely judge it to be her true policy to accept the position and maintain it. We have yet no proof that she has so soon become weary of the Union which, but a few years gone by, she so eagerly sought, and which has, in that short interval, heaped almost fabulous treasures into her lap. On the contrary, what proof we have presents her in the attitude of a hopeful friend of peace. We pray that she may prove steadfast to the admonitions of the wise and true hearted hero whom she has honored with the highest gifts she has had to bestow!

This is a brief survey of the materials which in the sad event of the disruption of our Confederacy, many suppose may be moulded into a united South. It exhibits two divisions of the present slaveholding States—separate, not hostile—but divided from each other by nature and incompatible conditions, impossible to be brought into harmonious alliance under any system of political organization founded upon the basis of what are deemed the essential and peculiar interests of either.

I have endeavoured to demonstrate my conviction that with whatever caution or friendly spirit of compromise they might begin the experiment of Confederation, they would infallibly lapse into antagonisms through the collision of which their association would soon be reduced to a mere political form, as impotent to hold them together as our present Union is likely to prove under the doctrines which one of the divisions I have mentioned above, has already proclaimed and adopted as the indispensable condition of its alliance.

Amongst many topics of discussion which would arise in the course of that experiment, there is one which would, certainly, loom into fearful proportions as a source of constantly increasing discontent. It is exemplified in our present history, and would find even a more acrimonious revival in the progress of the supposed new alliance.

The tendency of nearly all—perhaps I might say of the whole—of the Border States, in considerable portions or sections of each, must be under any form of organization—whether in the present Union or out of it; whether pursuing their own welfare united with the whole South, or in a Confederacy of their own— towards the increase of free labor by immigration and settlement, and to a correlative gradual diminution of slave labor. That process is marked out for them in the future, as it has been in the past, by the irresistible law of their nature. It is an onward force which derives its vigor from the stimulus of interest and is both the issue and the exponent of the prosperity of the community itself. In the grain-growing portions of these States, this process will be more rapid; but, even in the planting portions, though slower and perhaps for a time imperceptible, its influences will be felt. As population increases and the competition of labor becomes more intense, these States must expect a continuance of the same partial and progressive mastery of free over slave labor which is now visible in many local divisions of their own area, and which has been slowly and steadily converting slave into free States from the date of the Revolution down to the present time. Maryland, portions of Virginia, Kentucky and Missouri are moving onward to the final condition—remote but certain—of free labor communities. That movement may be greatly accelerated by extrinsic forces. The enhancement of the value of slaves draws this labor from a less productive to a more productive region—from the wheat to the cotton field. The depreciation of the value has, to some extent, a similar effect. By impoverishing the owner, it compels a necessity to sell, and the purchaser is most likely to be the agent or factor of the cotton planter. In either case the gradual decrease of slavery in the farming region—I use this designation in opposition to the planting—is the constant result. The establishment of the slave trade would not be without its effect in the same direction. It would create disgust in many against slavery itself, and thus lead to emancipation. These contingencies are entitled to consideration as causes which, in the lapse of time, may operate more or less actively upon the interests, habits, and sentiments of the Border States to produce not only a sharp diversity of views and policy, but also dissension and conflict between them and other sections of the South. They would grow to be reckoned as unfriendly to the South, or in the current phrase of our day, "unsound" on the question of Southern institutions. They would thus be regarded with a growing dislike, and, in the end, put to the ban of extreme Southern opinion, under the odious and comprehensive appellation of abolitionists.

Not in this question alone would be found a source of jealousy and division. Political ambition would contrive many pretexts for quarrel, and parties would vent their discontents in threats of secession and new combinations.

Disunion would find a terrible-precedent in the example of the present time, and grow to be the familiar and frequent threat, and often the actual deed of disappointed States. Mr. Jefferson long ago described this very condition of things. His words now reach us with solemn warning, as counsels sent to their erring sons from the sanctuary of our departed fathers. "In every free and deliberating society"— he says, in a letter to John Taylor, in the year 1798—"there must, from the nature of man, be opposite parties and violent discussions and discords; and one of these, for the most part, must prevail over the other for a longer or shorter time. Perhaps this party division is necessary to induce each to watch and delate to the people the proceedings of the other. But if, on a temporary superiority of the one party, *the other is to resort to a scission of the Union, no Federal Government can ever exist.* If to rid ourselves of the present rule of Massachusetts and Connecticut we break the Union, will the evil stop there? Suppose the New England States alone cut off, will our natures be changed? Are we not men still, to the South of that, with all the passions of men? Immediately we shall see a Pennsylvania and Virginia party arise in the residuary confederacy, and the public mind will be distracted with the same party spirit. What a game, too, will one party have in their hands, by eternally threatening each other, and unless they do so and so, they will join their Northern neighbors! If we reduce our Union to Virginia and North Carolina, immediately the conflict will be established between the representatives of these two States, and they will end by breaking into their simple units. Seeing, therefore, that an association of men who will not quarrel with one another, is a thing that never yet existed, from the greatest confederacy of nations down to a town meeting or a vestry; seeing that we must have somebody to quarrel with, *I had rather keep our New England associates for that purpose than to see our bickerings transferred to others.* * * * *A little patience, and we shall see the reign of witches pass over, their spells dissolved, and the people recovering their true sight, restoring their government to its true principles."*

We may commend both ~~to~~ the philosophy of these extracts and the prophecy with which they end, to the sober meditation of all who think the evils of the day incurable.

It is proper for me to say here that the propositions I have submitted as the foundation of a proper settlement, to be urged by the Border States, are but selections from the many suggestions which have in various forms been lately thrown before the public. I have selected these, not only because I think them altogether just, in view of the rational demands which both North and South are entitled to make upon each other, but also because they seem to have met a larger concurrence from the conservative portions of the people, on both sides, than any others that have been brought into discussion. A temperate debate of these propositions and their recommendation by the authority of a grave and influential convention of eminent citizens representing the moderate conservative opinion and the most important interests of the country—which I do not doubt greatly preponderate in both sections, and are quite able to outweigh and overmaster all the leaders and followers of the ultraisms of both—would, it strikes me, command, at once, the assent of the most authoritative mass of citizens, and gradually bring into submission, if not concurrence, the whole disturbing force which now distracts the public peace.

The advantage which the Border States hold in this controversy is very manifest. As I have said before, they are the masters of the position and may control the events of the future. It is in their power to isolate those portions of the Union which are most violent and reckless in driving the country to extremes, and thus give them occasion to perceive that they are to find no support out of the circle of their own impetuous allies. They have, also, the power to give, even to these, a strong assurance that every fair and just complaint they are entitled to make, shall be redressed by satisfactory arrangements which they, the Border States, will demand, and will most assuredly procure. The North will listen to their demands and meet them in honorable conference, with a temper of conciliation which it would be hopeless to expect from a conference representing the more excited and exacting portions of the South. We have proof of this temper furnished every day in the Northern journals. The abolitionists proper, the firebrands of the North, have lost their influence and would have no share in any movement towards a settlement. The truth is, that by far the greater number of the people of the Free States are awakened to a new perception of the danger which has been produced by the violent assaults of the North upon the South, in which they themselves have more or less participated without dreaming of the bitter injuries they were inflicting upon the public peace and the integrity of the Union. They have listened to evil counsellors and have been led away by the inflammatory philosophies of their own ambitious leaders. They see this now, although they have not seen it before ; and in this awakening of their minds to the reality of the crisis, they are ready and willing to make every proper concession for the restoration of present tranquility and for protection against future disturbance. They are thus fortunately able and well inclined to drop, henceforth and forever, this offensive and detestable agitation of slavery, which they now perceive to be a real and dangerous grievance.

Our purpose should be to negotiate with this class of men. It can be only effectually done by the Border States. A General Convention of all the States would, inevitably, produce more bickering and confusion in the present state of affairs. Even a General Convention, as has been proposed, of all the Southern States, with a view to their own course of proceeding, would be attended with the same difficulties. It would run the risk of being converted into a theatre of angry debate upon extreme propositions, and would be, as likely, as the Charleston Convention in May, to be broken up by the secession of discontented members who could not get all they asked. A Convention of the Border States would have no difficulty of this kind. They would be harmonious, just and reasonable in their views and firm in meeting the real evils of the time, by offering and demanding a full and adequate remedy for them.

5

This would be their position in the first efforts towards peace and permanent security. If they succeed in obtaining a just settlement, the seceding States could not resist the necessity of acquiescing in such a settlement, and of returning to the Union. As they calmed down into a cooler mood, and brought their unclouded judgment to a consideration of the case, they would cordially approve and support the settlement, and the whole country would thus receive an incalculable benefit from the present commotion. It would be a great and happy purification of the *morale* of the country, and we should all rejoice that the crisis has been turned to such good account.

But if this service, proffered by the Border States, should unhappily fail to produce these results, in this first stage of the process of pacification, they would still occupy a ground not less important and beneficial in the second and more remote phase of the quarrel.

Supposing a disintegration of the Union, notwithstanding all efforts to prevent it, to be forced upon us by the obstinacy and impracticability of parties on each side—the case would still be far from hopeless. The Border States, in that event, would form, in self-defence, a Confederacy of their own, which would serve as a centre of reinforcement for the reconstruction of the Union. The attraction of interest and good brotherhood would instantly become effective to draw to this nucleus, one by one, every State in the Confederacy. A beneficent power of gravitation would work with irresistible energy in bringing back the dislocated fragments. New York, New Jersey and Pennsylvania would be amongst the first to fall in. Illinois, Indiana, Ohio, perhaps all the Western States, would be unable to resist the tendency towards this centre, and would come into cohesion with an utter abjuration of all those fancies and follies which have been engendered by the slavery question. And when it was seen that North and South could thus unite on a basis perfectly free from the disturbance of these old questions, the more moderate of the seceding States—Georgia especially, if she be one of them,—would come to the acknowledgment that their true interests directed them to the same reunion. Last of all, the most ultra States of the secession movement would obey the same law of attraction, and, once more, after a lapse of weary trial and profitable experience, we should see the Union reconstructed by the healthful agency of the Border States.

Those who have carefully noted the progress of political opinion for more than thirty years past, and marked the tendency of its teaching, towards the adoption of certain distinctive theories of government having reference to supposed geographical interests, have been able to predict the certainty of a convulsion that, sooner or later, would present an inevitable necessity for a reconstruction or, at least, a reconsideration and explicit determination of the principles upon which the Union is to be preserved.

The present ferment is but the verification of this prediction.

If wisely handled, as I have shown, it may be productive of inestimable good. If allowed to solve its problem under the guidance of the fierce instincts and rash counsels of those who have first assumed its direction it will become the source of an "Iliad of woes"—not to the present generation alone, but to many generations hereafter.

The time and the occasion, therefore, demand the most free and full examination of the causes, open and concealed, which are shaking the loyalty of the people and turning men's thoughts towards disunion.

I have endeavored in these pages to demonstrate that there are other and more secret discontents in our condition, than those which grow out of the slavery question.

Whilst we painfully perceive and feel that the action of the Northern States on that question, and, still more, the wicked fanaticism of individuals and sects in preaching hostility to the peace of the South, have kindled in the mind of the whole population of this division of the United States, a profound and just indignation against this wanton spirit of aggression which, if not arrested, we have long been conscious, would surely lead to a rupture of the Union,—it is also a matter of deep concern that we should apprehend and notice the fact that there are other disturbing forces operating upon sections of the South—perhaps in some degree owing their vitality to the alienation produced by the slavery agitation, but now apart from it and looking to other subjects,—which have grown to be seriously hostile to the harmony of our united system of government. My aim has been to bring these into view, as well as the more pervading topic of discontent, in order that, in the attempt to restore peace and confidence, which is practicable through the settlement of the slavery dispute, we may not be misled by the clamor of those to whom such a settlement would be but the frustration of a cherished design. The dissatisfaction of this class of agitators must be left to the cure of time. There is no mode of treating it but to let it alone, consigning it to the good sense and right reason which it has to encounter at home.

It will, doubtless, be received as a bold assertion, when I say that the slavery question, as one for political cognizance in the United States, presents the most futile subject for legislation or administrative policy, perhaps, within the whole range of measures consigned to the notice of Government.

It cannot be controverted that the whole power of the Federal Government is inadequate to change the condition of a single slave within any State of the Union. Nor can any combination of party, with all the aids which the apparatus of Government may afford, with all the temper of pro-scription and intolerance that fanatical zeal may beget, with all the concurrence of sectional State legislation, ever be able to make a successful invasion of the rights of the smallest of the Slave States. Such an attempt would meet the instant resistance not only of the whole circle of those States, but with the resistance of three-fourths of the people of the whole country. That parties and individuals may threaten irre-pressible conflicts and undying hostility, is true. But, as to acting upon such threats, the Constitution renders them as powerless as children.

And in regard to slavery in the Territories—although there may be ground on which the Government may claim to control it, I affirm that, as a practicable policy, no exercise of that power, in the present actual condition of the domain possessed by the nation, can either force the establishment of slavery into a territory ungenial to it, nor keep it out of one adapted to its employment. I mean, that there is no motive of interest to take slavery, as a permanent thing, to a region where it is unproductive ; nor any motive, either political or philanthropic, to forbid its transfer to the region where it is essential to the interests of production. At this time we have no territory in which there is any possibility of raising the question, but if we should obtain one in a planting region, it would be settled from the population of the slaveholding States without a notable opposition from any section of the Union.

The agitation of slavery, therefore, notwithstanding its engrossment of the country and the odious prominence it has assumed, is, after all, but a parade of idle and mischievous debate. It lives upon the incessant ministration of stimulants supplied by small declaimers in quest of notoriety. It is, in the present generation, a moral epidemic which has seized upon whole districts, like St. Anthony's Dance in the fourteenth century. The fancy of getting up "a great abomination," in order to turn it to account as a topic of popular preaching, is as old as the first consecrated cobbler. Nor, is it at all a new thing to set up a popular sin to be extirpated by law. Many quack politicians have been wasting their energies for years, upon the abortive attempt to legislate peaceable families into the disuse of spirituous liquors, by bringing alcohol into platforms and making parties upon it:—but alcohol has gained the day and the Maine Liquor Law has become a dead letter. The world laughs at this prodigality of ineffectual zeal. May we not learn to treat with quiet scorn the more malignant but still impotent ebullitions of the sanctimonious vanity of New England ?

In truth, slavery has not, in itself—I mean African slavery

as now existing in the United States—the condition for any vehemently honest indignation against it ; nor, on the other side, for any vehemently honest affection for it. It is, simply, a very appropriate and necessary agent in the interests of civilization, where it is; and would be, generally, a very wretched thing where it is not. The wrath that is stirred against it, and the patriarchal beauty that is claimed for it, are both the offspring of excited imaginations. African slavery, in this country, at least, is, for the most part, a clear gain to the savage it has civilized. Whatever it may be to others, it has been a blessing to *him*. It is also clearly a blessing to Massachusetts, and to England, France, Germany. But, it is a very doubtful blessing to the master who has charged himself with the solicitude of supporting, employing and caring for the slave ; it is, at best, but a mixed and greatly diluted blessing to him. Strange, that those who enjoy the unmixed blessing of sharing the profits of slavery, should be the rancorous conspirators against the peace of him who takes all its burthens and hazards upon himself !

The true solution of all this extravagance is, that the importance given to the questions evolved by the slavery excitement, is the mere artifice of politicians. Our slavery would have slept quiet under the surface of society, until the day of its appointed term, if it had not been found serviceable as a figure for the arena of politics. Unfortunately, it is a topic of singular capability for either a discourse in the pulpit or a speech upon the stump ; the most fruitful for exaggeration, the most sensitive for alarm. It has proved to be a "drawing" theme for sensation parsons in pursuit of popularity ; for sensation politicians in pursuit of the Senate ; for speculative editors who are anxious to increase their subscription lists by means of pious politics and cheap philanthrophy. It has shown itself capable of converting atrabilious tradesmen into governors, legislators and judges; and of lifting up innumerable apprentices, journeymen, colporteurs and pedagogues to the elevation of shining lights in the Conventicle. It has fired the soul of many a cross-road orator of the "sunny South" with indignant and eloquent wrath against universal Yankeedom; and given birth to scores of conventions and thousands of resolutions, to expound the Constitution on the theory that its authors did not know what they were about.

Then, again, it has furnished to strong-minded women, who have declared their independence of the petticoat, an occasion for an equally heroic abnegation of the prejudice of color, and so to bring, both pantaloons and amalgamation, into their bill of rights.

It has, over and over again, supplied a conclave of crazy fanatics, in the orgies of their anniversaries, with an opportunity to denounce the Union as a Covenant of Hell, and the Bible and the Constitution as a double curse to mankind. It has, on the other hand, wrought the remarkable effect of diverting hot-headed young politicians from their newspapers, to the study of the Scriptures, to find texts in the Pentateuch and the Epistles of Paul, to convict the whole North of the iniquity of blaspheming the "divine institution."

It has done all this and a thousand times as much, but it has never yet succeeded in establishing a single point for which it has professed to contend, nor accomplished a single result at which slavery would not have sooner arrived, if left to the silent evolution of its own destiny:—always excepting, from this denial of its doings, that solitary achievement—in which its success has been perfect—the opening of a Pandora box of murder, rapine, implacable hatred and revenge.

It has made and defeated Presidents, cabinets and diplomatists, has got up wars and annexations, built and destroyed platforms; but it has been utterly impotent to arrest the steady increase of slave labor, or its transfer to whatever region it has been found profitable to remove it. So far from promoting lawful emancipation, or checking either the growth or productiveness of slavery, it has wholly arrested the first, and has witnessed the augmentation of the value of the slave and the profits of his work a hundred fold since the agitation began.

These are the chief triumphs and these the failures of a slavery agitation of thirty years, conducted by men claiming to be intellectual, conscientious and stricken with a conviction that it is the great and paramount duty of the age to reform, what they have wrought themselves to believe, the damning sin of a nation. For this, clergymen who think they have "a mission," spouters who think themselves orators, and politicians who think themselves statesmen, have gone on laboring all these thirty years, in the same ceaseless and fruitless routine of sermons, conventions and pamphlets—vexing the heart of the South with vulgar vituperation and insult, and ruffling the temper of Congress with silly petitions to do impossible things, showered, in endless profusion of repetition, from the kitchens and primary schools and factories of New England.

So far as the agitation kept within the limits of this phase of its career, it was comparatively harmless. It could only provoke, but could not sting. In the language of the reviewer I have quoted above—"it could but make us angry." The South, indeed, are to blame for their loss of temper under this provocation; as that really afforded the assailants the only gratification they had. It would have been wiser to treat it, as more self-possessed nations are accustomed to treat the extravagancies of fanaticism; as we ourselves, indeed, now treat Mormonism or free love or the nonsense of Fourierism.

But the agitation, in the last few years, has become venomous. It has directed its activity towards disunion and destruction of the Government. Finding that the pretence of conscientious regard for law, and action within the pale of the statutes, cramped its benevolent designs, it changed its tactics and entered into a more congenial career,—devoting its energy to a plot for illegal and even treasonable disturbance, by enlisting companies and providing facilities for stealthy abduction of slaves, by provoking servile insurrection, and by armed incursions against the peace of communities within the slaveholding region : whilst, at the same time, it solicited and won the co-operation of many States to this organized plan of felony, so far as to obtain from them the passage of laws to nullify the provision of the Constitution and the statutes of the National Legislature for the recovery of the fugitives which might escape or be abducted from the South.

This is the second and recent phase of the agitation. Could any sensible man in the North suppose, that a union of our States was at all possible, if this system of assault and disturbance were recognized and sustained by any respectable or authoritative opinion in the Free States? Could any one imagine, that if such a system of annoyance should receive the sanction of legislative bodies, of conventions representing a predominant power in any State, of religious communities, of parsons holding a grade above a crazy fanatic, of professors of colleges, lawyers, merchants or gentlemen of any weight in society—in short, of any portion of Northern society that might be regarded as the exponent of the common opinion of the community—and not inevitably and inexorably force upon the whole South, not only the desire but the duty to retire from a compact of union with all such States as fostered such an agitation? Between independent nations, such provocations would be the instant and just cause of war, and no nation, with the power to protect its own peace and honor, would hesitate to vindicate itself in that way.

This later scheme of aggression presents the first earnest and effective movement towards disunion, which has been made outside of the seceding States. The Free States which have encouraged, or co-operated in, this scheme, may claim whatever credit there is, in being the first to set the ball of disunion in motion. The Border States, though the chief sufferers from these attacks, have been loyal to the Constitution and Union, when these agitators have been recreant.

When the Republican party was organized in the bosom of this agitation, and abstract and useless speculations, touching the control of slavery by the Federal Government, were brought into the political field by both parties, to heighten and embitter the feud between the two sections ; when all the prestige and power of organized political forces predominant in the popular vote of the Union, were enlisted in battle array against the South; when a President and Vice-President, contrary to all previous usage, were selected from the same section to represent it; and when this new embodiment was heralded to the country, with proclamation that its purpose was the administration of the Government towards the enforcement of the theory of an irrepressible conflict with slavery, until every vestige of it should be banished from the Republic; and that the aid of a higher law than the Constitution should be sought for the ratification of the act,—was there not enough to propagate a wide and fearful alarm throughout the whole South for the safety, not only of its property, but of its very existence?

The systematic abduction of slaves, through organized Northern agencies, is already sequestering a million of Southern wealth every year. The final consummation of this movement to the destruction of slavery, would be the sequestration of two or three thousand millions of that wealth. It would be to turn several States back into a jungle for wild beasts. It would be to paralyze the industry and subtract one-half from the comforts of Europe and America. Is it at all wonderful that now, when that party has succeeded and has elected its President, that the alarm of the South should be increased, and that the Southern States should feel that a crisis had been forced upon them which is to determine whether we can have a Union in peace—or peace without a Union?

These are the true sources of alarm to the South, and these the questions which the people there earnestly believe they have to solve.

If it were really true that the whole North were united in this scheme of aggression, then, indeed, the case would be hopeless. Hundreds of thousands in the South—the great majority of the people—believe this to be so. But, it is not true. Happily, it is not true. The belief is the delusion by which the Southern mind has been cruelly abused: abused by credulous and ardent politicians; by selfish demagogues; by a prejudiced and, sometimes, by a wicked press; by the politicians of party, who hope to find in the wreck of society something serviceable to the reconstruction of their power.— No, it is not true that these are the purposes of any portion of the Free States, worthy of a moment's consideration as a force to influence the current of Government. Threefourths—I might say nine-tenths—of the people of the Free States are as guiltless of any imagining against the rights of the South, or its peaceful enjoyment of its own pursuits, as the people of the South themselves. Any one acquainted with the real opinion of the North will say, that the masses, in those States, are profoundly unconscious of the tendency of the doctrines of which they have heard so much, towards any serious assault upon the South. Their prurient tastes have been fed to plethora, with stories of the barbarism of slavery; and, naturally enough, they believe that it is a very bad thing;—but as to meddling with it, further than going to hear a lecture upon it by the Rev. Mr. Pepperpot, and to feast upon his spiced flummery, they have not the least wish or purpose. As to dissolving the Union for it!—they open their eyes to an incredulous stare, and wont, even now, believe that there is a man in the United States so insane as to dream of such a thing.

To the conception of all this mass, constituting the whole real power of the Free States, the Republican party and the Republican President are but the regular successors to the administration of the Government which, in their belief, is to be conducted in the old fashion of attending to the business of the country, to the preservation of the Union, and to giving as much content as possible to every section and every interest in the country.

They are quite ready—I speak now of the people, and not of the politicians; the latter have already proved themselves to be Incapables, and the matter will have to be taken out of their hands—these masses are now quite ready to make any arrangements, constitutional or conventional, which may be found necessary for peace. They will come to any reasonable agreement upon intervention or non-intervention, squatter or non-squatter sovereignty, protection or non-protection of slavery in the territories,—without the attempt to unriddle these jargons,—that may be found requisite for the restoration of good temper and good will amongst the States. *They will do any thing to save the Union on principles adapted to make it perpetual.* It will not be three months before that will be the whole creed of the Republican party. Let the South be assured of this.

The first duty of conciliation lies on the side of that party. Let the North dismiss its obstinacy and its silence, and come, with its customary shrewdness, to doing the right thing. Get slavery out of that gigantic and tenacious conscience of theirs, which is such a voracious absorbent of other people's sins, and fill its place with Christian charity, and love of its neighbor, and other forgotten virtues, and we shall then find some returning sunshine. But let the Free States every where, and the sober, reflective and honest men in them, understand, that *the old Union is an impossibility unless the agitation of slavery is brought to an end.*

There is nothing in the election of Mr. Lincoln which may now be regarded as an obstacle to this pacification. With whatever apprehension many may have allowed themselves to anticipate, from that election, the inauguration of a policy which would be one of continual exasperation, it is very evident, now that the election is over and the views of the new President are becoming known through the best accredited organs of the party he represents, that there is no reason to fear his administration will not be conducted with a salutary and becoming respect for the rights and interests of every portion of the country. Indeed, from the date of the nomination of Mr. Lincoln, the presages of political events have all been favorable to a better hope of the future, than we might gather from the pernicious zeal and intemperate proclamation of those who assumed to be the leading champions and most authentic expounders of the principles of his party.

His nomination was both a surprise and a disappointment to, what may be termed, the most demonstrative portion of the Republican party. He was selected as the more eligible candidate, in the belief that he would attract a support from States and large masses of the people who were not willing to adopt the extreme views upon which his rival for the nomination was put forward. And, in the eventual trial, he was elected, in great part, by a vote representing rather an opposition to the democratic, than a concurrence with the distinctive and exceptionable principles of the Republican party. In other words, Mr. Lincoln was both nominated and elected by what may be called the moderate, conservative division of the Republican party. And it is now claimed for him,—and apparently with his own approbation,—that he stands before the people of the United States unembarrassed by the extreme pretensions which were set up for the party in the canvass; and that he will enter into office, not only with the determination, but with the desire to render his administration one of impartial justice to the South.

There is, at least, a good omen in this, and the strongest motive for an appeal to the South to wait for more explicit demonstration of the policy of the coming administration.

If the seceding States, in their zeal for a separate confederacy, are not willing to wait for this demonstration, it will be justly regarded by the world, as a confession that the revolution in which they have embarked has only been promoted, but, not originated by the event upon which they have heretofore placed its justification.

If *they* are not willing to wait, the Border States will not be shaken from their resolves to wait and avail themselves of every favorable incident that may be turned to the account of peaceful adjustment.

Upon the new President, will then devolve the responsibility of bringing the influence of the government, and the weight of his own admonition and example, to the duty of defining and determining (if that be not successfully done by his friends before his inauguration) the pledges which his party are disposed to give for the permanent establishment of friendly relations between the two sections of the Union.

We have no reason to doubt that Mr. Lincoln's influence to this end will be propitious to peace. It will then be seen that, in the position assumed by the Border States; in their firmness, justice and dignified bearing throughout this controversy, they will have become the authoritative and controling power to devise and establish the foundations of a secure and durable settlement, with every provision for the preservation of Southern rights which the seceding States themselves could reasonably demand.

MARYLAND, *December* 17, 1860.

ERRATUM.—On page 32, first line, "we commend both to," strike out "*to.*"